Confident Music Would Fly Us to Paradise

Confident Music Would Fly Us to Paradise

Carol Levin

To DANCey with WARm Regards
To A Fallon Poet

Carol Levin
9/21/14

MoonPath Press

Poetry
ISBN 978-1-936657-15-5

Cover photo by Rolf Konow
From the film *The Magic Flute* by Kenneth Branagh
Used by courtesy of the Peter Moores Foundation
and Ideale Audience
photo © Ideale Audience

Author photo by Jeffery Bassuk

Book design by Tonya Namura
using Cochin

MoonPath Press is dedicated to publishing the
best poets of the U.S. Northwest Pacific states

MoonPath Press
PO Box 1808
Kingston, WA 98346

MoonPathPress@yahoo.com

http://MoonPathPress.com

This book is dedicated to Seattle Opera.

This company has had an immeasurable impact on my life. Seattle Opera brings the magnitude of opera's artistic quality and professionalism not only to Seattle but to the world community.

Music is the gift my mother, Jeanette Horn Fogelson, gave me. Not only did she fill the house with music from the phonograph, she trained to sing operatic roles. However, her dream of singing opera, sadly, never got further than when she sang while washing dinner dishes. But I was there. She has been in my thoughts, singing, all through the long process of composing my poems.

Later, Seattle Opera offered me a significant opportunity by including me in the company for twenty years as a "super," on stage in silent roles.

Carol Levin

Gratitude and Appreciation

I am sincerely grateful for the support and guidance offered by wonderful poets: Jeannine Hall Gailey, Christine Johnson-Duell, and Diane Lockward. I thank Karren Alenier for the generous gifts of her time and intelligence.

Mountains of thanks to my diligent poet colleagues, Vicki Ford, Ruth Brinton, Neile Graham and Katie Tynan.

An encore thank you to Patricia Fargnoli, my early mentor-teacher, for vigorously encouraging me to include my experience performing in operas as inspiration for poems.

With a fanfare ovation: I continue to give everlasting appreciation and admiration to Lana Hechtman Ayers, the publisher, editor of MoonPath Press, whose open-hearted spirit and boundless enterprise brings so much encouragement to me, to the world of poetry, poets and to all writers.

I offer all my gratitude to Pierre-Olivier Bardet, of Idéale Audience who granted me the privilege of using my cover photo and the extraordinary artist, Rolf Konow, of Still Photography, who took the photo promoting Kenneth Branagh's film, *The Magic Flute*.

And always, I am grateful to my family Ari Steinberg, Suzanne DeWitt, Aylee Welch, Kai Welch and Sage Welch. And forever, to my dearest love, Geo.

Acknowledgments

My thanks to the editors and publishers of the following periodicals and books where these poems first appeared some in slightly different versions:

Avatar Review: "Wild Wishes"

Grey Sparrow Journal: "You Sing in Your Sleep Too"

Junctures: The Journal for Thematic Dialogue: (Dunedan, NZ) "We Don't Sing Carols in Our House"

Red Ochre Literary Press: "Destiny's Obbligato Perseveres" earlier version titled "Destiny Watches With His Shoulders Back and Head Craned Forward"

String Poet: "Robert Davidson, Trapeze Dancer"

the Mom Egg: "The Chambers in Symphony Hall"

The Red Headed Stepchild: "There's No Right Way to Do This Wrong"

Verse Wisconsin: "First Flight to Denver"

The Tampa Review: Mark Morris: Paul Hindemith, *Kammermusik No. 3*

Table of Contents

Yet through the silence something throbs, and gleams...
—Antoine de Saint-Exupéry, *The Little Prince*

Confident
Music Would Fly
Us to Paradise

One

Growing Up: an Old Fashioned
Circus Act Opera

This is how I remember it now.
My silence waits where there's a barber's pole,
a painted wooden lighthouse, the reflection
of light on a front door, a closed window waiting.
Could be I'm a delicate red bird ready to fly.
Circling in a baby-buggy sized car,

could be, I'm the *auguste* clown: loud stripes
mismatched, undersized collar, oversized shoes,
inaudible and invisible, where in the back seat more
clowns costumed as thirty pairs of chickadees nest
along with life's minutia marking time.

Our opera's a circus spiel, augmented chorus and calliope.
Our opera's clown-mobile roars to rest and we pour out.
An expanding shadow
shaped like a moving octopus: arms and arias,
a glister of voices set free. My own hovers aflutter.

Ida LaGray Elucidates How Long Love Can Last Before It Is Severed

Andrea Chénier

Evokes my antediluvian
    adolescence
stealing away
to marry
    an exotic
tenor sax, confident
music
    would fly us to paradise — by the eleventh hour

I'm *Ida LaGray* caught in an arc
of follow-light and shadow, my nightmare
    is prison, act four,
where I wait
for the *national razor*
    to shatter sleep.

In an earlier act
the Revolutionary rabble chorus
    hurls raw vegetables
cabbage, carrots, even apples
across the stage
    bulls-eyes at me
Ida LaGray entering

from upstage
facing down
    the opera's mock trial.
Ida LaGray's
a condemned token of her adolescent
    self, her nocturnal unease
conceals her brain will still desire
and eyes weep after the blade beheads.

She sits next to the big body
of the tenor
    Ben Heppner
who, a year later
loses his ruffled shirt
    voice, his dreams in a heap.
But now singing *Chénier*, he's the poet caught
in chaos, revolution,
    and love —

When *Chénier's* lover sings her last words in the last act:
"This is not farewell but an end to suffering,"
    they jolt, like all jolts, the guillotine's slick rap.

Mostly, Silence

with Frankie Laine
and Nat King Cole. No
sound, no voice. But the *Hit
Parade* and Saturday's
radio opera diverted
cat's-got-yer-tongue?
Often, barefoot soles of feet,
head, torso, arms
and legs leaping substituted
for words.

Paused, afraid strange
step-brother Jerry
would talk, but no sound.
Except the step-father
and my mother vibrating
the bedroom wall —
she was crying
he was yelling
softly. No sound

except Celene
and I after
school, smearing toast
with honey, sipping Lipton's
from flowered teacups.
Her widow's peak, high
forehead and smarts
my unspoken envy. No
sound in class when
I was called.
No sound, I could
not make sound, not a sound,
other than, when my mother

yelled, hollered
and I made

as much sound
back. A lot of sound, loud.
I yelled and yelled at her

at the very moment
the radio sang
When you walk through a storm hold your head up high
and I cried sound down
my cheeks, mother
never heard it.

The Ruin of What We Said

I search for anything said about silence:
someone said, "soundlessness is peaceful."
Someone said, "silence is mute dumbness."
Someone said, "hush."
I heard myself say, "death." Death?

"Silence propagates itself, and the longer
talk has been suspended, the more
difficult it is to find anything to say,"
says Samuel Johnson.
His friend says, "an outburst inside
pressurizes fear
so swallow silence."
Someone said, "*mew*, to move air."

Someone said, "before deciding
on action take soundings
to keep from going aground
on a sea-mined sandy shoal."
I would have said, "don't make waves."
Someone feared "sounding like
a bugling bull elk rutting." Rutting?

I search for anything
to drop a heavy
line to measure bottom waves of circulation,
my blood pumps
a backwash of unexplored sea.

Someone said, "sounding out a word."
Someone said, "lifts off in sighs."
Everyone said, "it's innate."
Someone said, "huh."
Like baby's tongue twisting
in her first foray

of knee and hand
foreword to crawl
I search a way to speak peace with you.

The Makeup Artist Makes Up Me

Bending close
applying an alchemy
of verisimilitude
you say *close please*.

A palette:
    handing
myself
to your hands
brushes, tubes
and tubs of foundation
bases and powders
highlights and shadows
concealer, rouge and blush
blossoming on light pink cheeks.

Lip, eye liner and lashes last.
Your fingers tug
wrapping my white warp
of netted pin curls,
with caramel-colored
real-hair ringlets.

The spell cast
is released to breathe
after so long. Incantations
of myselves proliferate.

Dressed to boogie
with an airy heart
in a churning sea
I burst out in eerie language
of ancient children.

Dear Director, It's *Werther* This Season

Eminent Director. Last
time, just for you she studied
every gesture, memorized
movements then froze upstage:
you tempered her
in illuminated intensity,
angles and colors, your tornado
of sarcasm bellowed, *stupid lady*!

She'd missed that production's
weather warning
when she agreed
to your off-beat scheme
for light-walking Debussy's
Pelléas et Mélisande.
Today like a dust devil
the old memory recalled

is suddenly severe-clear
in backstage gloom, the smell,
the stagehand's nod evoking
old tidal-waves of Tech Week's
pins and needles days,
bone-aching nights
when she prepped the premiere
onstage, center stage, solitary
in the light dimming
as *Mélisande* died.

Money men, New York reporters,
and stage crew, took notes rating
her in your chip-on-the shoulder

experiment. She braced herself
by quoting William Cullen Bryant:
    "A whirling ocean that fills the wall
    Of the crystal heaven, and buries all.
    And I, cut off from the world, remain
    Alone with the terrible hurricane."

Irked under the thunder
of her reappearance in *Werther*
Herr Director, you're the same
old forecast, your tweeds
and receding brow.
But now she knows you, poor baby,
when this time she's costumed
as the nursemaid nanny, and you
analyze *The Sorrows*
of Young Werther, an advisory
based on Goethe's early life
of convoluted love.

At opera's end before *Werther* dies
there is a shift in atmospheric pressure
lit like the Aurora Borealis
as *Charlotte* consoles *Werther*
by declaring her love and *Werther*
begs forgiveness. He inspires
you, oh Blustery Director, as you lift
the low pressure trough by offering
your apology in a local region
of clearing, overdue.

Two

A Time of Tiny Terrors

Remain. In readiness: hours of waiting, wait your

turn until something

happens, loiter, linger, twiddle thumbs, hang fire to

mark time, be ready

to be ready, (no whistling backstage) delay,
interlude, intermission, on break,

a point in the journey where one continues

to pause. Hesitation

heightens drama.

The call.

Stage Manager points: Places please   ready:

go!!   birthing   catch it.

My *butterflies* thought "go"

would paralyze. When we think back to stare on

both sides our image

is reversed as we fly into lights,   inferno   ablaze,
life force,   creatures of the stage.

The Prop Bag Needed a Body

Rigoletto

Stifling in a burlap bag on a stage floor. Dragged in the
bag on my back ablaze

with fury at my delighted mother
who may have been revamped as the *Duke's*

deep bodice courtesan. I'm unruly
as any twelve year old can be, being dragged

to *perform* in an *opera*. It might
not be true but my singer mother said

I was doubling in the bag for Lily Pons
singing Gilda, whose dying last act

hit high notes the audience swooned
over. Truth is I saw her, from under my gunny,

already laid-out onstage after
her character's last note drifted

to the stage-right chutes.
Weeping, her misshapen

father, Rigoletto, bends by her body
singing his last sad song

as Pons, supposedly dead,
in cahoots with me, revolts,

suddenly bending her knees
to an audience response I can't

remember. After all I was a child
and could barely lie still for laughing.

Storm

I fear the sound of thunder:
all I heard is Harold
wanted to name me
Carol, a sonancy of
Harold
and Jeannette wanted
to name me Annette
a reverberation of Jeanette.

I fear the flash of lightning:
all I can surmise
is how jagged name-
calling must have been.
Conceivably I kicked,
wrapped wailing
in the layette.

I fear the interval from flash to bang:
how uneasy the birth
certificate squiggled
the pact of Carol Ann.

I fear the side door blowing off:
as something slit
the bond when Harold Seymour
dispatched himself leaving only
his echo

in the trio as prelude and fugue:
fearing hearts drained of love
myself as conductor
doubling in the ensuing years —
Carol Carol Carol Harold.

First Flight to Denver

A stranger, some family friend
extending a favor, passed
the small paper bag from the seatpocket
on the ascent over the Rockies.
I swallowed back but heaved.

Chagrined and silent we waited,
shoulder to shoulder to land.

The 1946 June night was flat
against the window and as always,
I wrapped myself in quiet.
This silence was the worst, that taste
soiled my lips, I didn't dare lift my eyes.

The propeller finally stopped,
the DC-3 door

clanked as it was lifted.
Head spinning I descended
to the tarmac to my father
shadowy against the lights.
He was a stranger, we hadn't yet met.

I was small for ten, so he knelt
to my height held my hand, skimmed

my cheek, his cool lips and a narrow
brown mustache —
Then he stood,
said thank-you with a handshake.
My companion disappeared
through the terminal's glass door
without a backward glance.

Madama Butterfly's Mother

Whispering *oh no*, as hems
of our kimonos snag shuffling
along the rough raked stage,

pit orchestra commences
the wedding entrance,
chorus a color wheel
of parasols in pastels.

I'm the mother
flanked onstage
by two sopranos
fixing on our mark.
Same sopranos
at act's end sympathetically

but emphatically drag me,
unwilling to leave the sobbing
newlywed-child, on a terrace
above Nagasaki harbor.

Eyes on the conductor
Cio-Cio-San the bride
a tender fifteen,
soon to be damned by
a high priest's curse
gazes demurely down, bows
to her American *Pinkerton*.

The Official looks
to me, singing. Looks
to me, her *mother*.
His aria requires
my wedding blessing.
I incline assent

on the precise note
thinking, every night,
no, If I nod No
oh no, I will upend
the outcome
of this entire opera.

The Opera House Hall of Changing Rooms

Handmaidens to the singspiel
Queen of the Night or caretakers

of lives terminated by *Turandot*. Transmogrified
from libretto tales we're attired

in our room on the top floor full of racks hustled
up four stories of steep ramps, garments muscled

along by wardrobe designers, stitchers and measurers
    squinting
to catch torn armpits, wild threads, missing tights, bad
    hats,

and tinfoil gemstones. They scrutinize our checklist taped
to our dressing room mirror. *Dressers* ready to zip, lace
    and tie us in.

Facing reflections, torsos twist to glimpse our own backs
as tummies twitter opening-night. Little gifts and cards
    litter —

safety pins, bobby pins, vials of deodorant. Chatter chirps
above liquidy warm-ups floating from floors below:

baritones, sopranos, contraltos and tenors pitch scales
and waves of arias up.

Strings bow an A, the timpani tunes a tangle unraveling
when meekish Walter Mitty crawls from his fourth-floor
    clanking

green dragon scales to set the world of *Sigfried* aflame
    defying
the breach between daily life's hole of sadness. We veer

like peacocks swiveling our plumes of incandescent eyes
churned by the exchange of energy with the audience

Suzanne and I Were Cast

together. Lady's maids to La Marquise
in *The Daughter of The Regiment*. Onstage
    a matched set in black
floor-length long-sleeved
    Australian wool dresses, adorned
with tidy white pinafores. White
    bonnets resemble outrageous
lace soufflés. Her character
    is cast as the undermaid
under the thumb of my seniority.
    Under those high hats and hot
dresses we're soaked
    in perspiration under hot
stagelight. Offstage I am Suzanne's
    mother-in-law. Mother-in-law:

a title the brunt of comedians
    and *old boys* in bars. I just
heard one say his "mother-in-law
    looked her best in an urn,"
then came a cacophony of guffawing, beating
    thighs with pleasure.
I start to sweat when research
    reveals, Romans, in their era
slapped the same target for fun. Throughout
    the opera's convoluted story the daughter
of the regiment's a daughter mothered only
    by an army of fathers, under a threat
of becoming daughter-in-law
    to the mother
of the man she doesn't love.

Wild Wishes

I wished for a black tango clinging
to my thighs in a smoky Brazilian bar,
I wished to be Tosca catching
ovations of roses at the Met.
Wished to be the fire eater
in the Barnum and Bailey.

    At eighteen Father funds
the little apartment I wish for.
Green and naive my grandiose
adventure fizzles. I dream eternal
romance, my runaway
wedding bores the justice
of the peace. I was the kid
too scared to climb trees.
Mother, unconvinced wishes
I wasn't so wild.

I read once, "Knowing what to wish for
is as elusive as the delicate
blue-green orb of Neptune rising
at sunset, a ball of hydrogen
with rings we can't see."

In the wishing days I'd never
have deemed
today's life a life
to long for.
Never would have wished blue sky
this serene, sea lions singing me to sleep,
children and grandchildren
at baseball yesterday, cheering
together in the pleasure
of each other's pleasure.

Couldn't have dreamt your clashing
clothes and shaggy beard.
You, who came to me so late, so late,
you: holding out your hand—
any time I wish.

Unreliable Sensory Appreciation

"So you think you're changed do you?"
"I'm afraid I am, Sir," said Alice "I can't
remember things as I used—and I don't keep the
same size for ten minutes together"
— Lewis Carroll

❊❊

I feel like my arm is out on a limb this afternoon in a
thicket of soiled laundry: measuring dialogue feeling like
Alice silently shrinking above tangled sleeve and shorts,
that in any language whisper intimacy in a ghost's voice.
And there is ghostly fragrance of slept-in white sheets
wrinkled as though bending down heads to hide smiles.

❊❊

The clock bumped its hands forward beginning this
day exquisite as a day different in size when I rolled
over flinging my right arm onto a plain of emptiness.
A fling into spring's light, appearing later than it did
yesterday but staying on longer. Everything seems to
have changed.

❊❊

Only minutes before high noon I flail in poke-holes of my
own slip-ups escalating literary nonsense in the agitating
smutty piles of winter arm-pits in blue work shirts and
dingy tighty-whities, after asking what the next excess
of action or slight solitude of moment will bring.

❊❊

And spring delivers its nosegays grinning in scrubbed
corners. If only, I wished, I could feel as guilt free hiding
in my short memory. But then, the same as Alice years
afterward I bring the whole scene back again like a ghost
in his haunt and it feels, surely, like it was just yesterday.

I Want to be Martha Graham

Glancing backward leaping
trajectories

    of curvilinear ribbons,
    movements of

        muscles quivering when
        I think with my brain,

            bones, organs and flesh,
            eventually worn threadbare by overuse.

                I ascend from all directions drifting
                right to right, have the trick

                    of sideways seeing later softened
                    with bags under my eyes. Still, can
                     you see

                my hips move like platens
                of continents slipping side to side?

            By default I understand I'm just a daughter
            of this eccentric danseuse, a quivering

        little snipper-snapper growing slender
        dreaming lithe, taking pains

    in a vocabulary of fall and recovery.
    And although I yes, please,

thank-you and smile
until my teeth tire out

            compulsion can't conceal I'm an impostor
            fluttering torso to tush.

Abruptly unveiled I'm
a birthday sparkler's

    phosphoresce exposed
    by voluptuous time. Do you agree,

        oh Goddess of Venus, that I appear
        to be, yes, unmistakably, yes

            just me, an old broad
            in the pink, dancing?

Eloquence

If you refrain
  speaking
    for yourself
      speaking your mind
        in tongues
          speaking out
            volumes
              speaking frankly
              do you
                sing instead
                no
                  you dance

Three

Lights Out, Curtain Closed, It Begins

Das Rhinegold

Although he's dead deliberately
he manipulates this extra long darkness

to ensure gossip will subside
with a shuffle of coughs, a settling-in.

Under its weight you're seized
by the magnetic field of Wagner's silence

forcing you to leave everything
in the lighted world behind.

He makes you forsake harsh car honks
and potholes, he frees you

from gridlock's green, rapid yellow
and unresponsive red, puts to rest

anxiety flashes, to-do lists,
forgets and failures. You wave to

years flashing on, rush to conclude
all goodbyes. He impels surrender

sets you adrift
on an inhale of the baton.

Drenched in darkness separated
from gravity palpated by Wagner's

double-bass' insistent opening E note
lengthening like a lifeline, aerating

into an octave, he offers no inkling
of the world about to be revealed

in music's mingling colors, until bass-
viols and the audience

are out of breath and the whole earth cracks
as strings strafe flexing the pitch like a rolling red tide.

Swollen With Music

clutching coats and keys we sigh
through the portal forced into raw traffic,

beset by monotone voices, sirens, shifting lights on wet
streets, compelled to take back, like old baggage, our own
   lives.

& Fate Nestles Among the Chorus

I am my world.
—Wallace Stevens, from
"Bantams in Pine-Woods"

I live onstage in the character's circumstances

surrounded by
air just air
articulating —

within human instruments.

Sound waves bounce
dominating acoustic cavities
the frequencies
of each voice's 3000 hertz
undulate harmonic motion.

Isn't that remarkable

resonance, articulation,
flexibility & vibrato.

We don't need to know

the position of the tongue, the loosening &
   tightening
of the vocal folds the exertion
of the muscular thrust.

I am a receptacle being vibrated

my system changed
circulation exalted.
Life for this moment is electrified sensation.

Not at all like dying.

The Relatives in *My* Libretto

The characters feel like real people.
You sympathize with them; you want
everything to work out . . .
—Stephen Maus

(a basso buffo) Here's my Grampa Horn
taking a bow.

Never spoke at home. Pitched a line
of products on the road soliciting sales.
Horsey long chin stretched into his only laugh
in a lifetime the day he turned the garden hose away
from a pile of fresh caught fish, took aim
and soaked my starched dress, face, arms and legs,
the seven year old daughter of his daughter
pretending to sing *Pore Jud is daid*.

(contralto) Here's Granny Elizabeth,
taking a bow.

She hired the help, wore hats to temple,
crocheted and embroidered, but sealed
her lips until they were blue, silent
to the intruder who grew up in her home,
practicing make-believe Ziegfield Follies flappers
behind Granny's flowery living-room chair.

(contertenor) Here's Granny & Grampa's son
taking a bow.

Soaking eczema in a bathtub of oatmeal
he scented the entire house.
The rest of the time Uncle Willie scratched
in a back bedroom he seldom left.
He might have been young but raw and red,

avoiding my presence as I relished
the mishmashed words to *Mairzy Doats*.

    (coloratura soprano) Here's Auntie Ruth
    taking her bow.

Charming in her social smile
arranging parties, baking lamb-shape
coconut cakes and sewing me double-circle
skirts thinking I was misbegotten,
while I was secretly singing *Hey Good Lookin,
whatcha got cookin* . . . carefully
sidestepping Auntie Ruth's rivalry
with her sister, my mother.

    (basso profondo) Here's Uncle Ernie:
    Bowing.

Swash, the sound of a straight-edge
sharpening on a thick strop gave shape
to a massive black mustache.
Shouting over his shoulder
he threatened to "trim the tails" of his
two boisterous boys, while silently
I moved my lips mouthing
My Defenses Are Down.
But he let me be.

    (dramatic soprano) Mommy, who was poor,
    bows.

Outcast and homely she sang opera
and loved. Loved illicitly.
I'm a braided daughter in pj's
holding the alarm to her
earring'd ears every morning
puffing-up air to the tune of *Many a New Day*

    (non-singing role) Here's me, applauding.

I wove make-believe and music into silence
like a silk safety net. *Doin' What Comes Naturally*!

I Carried a Torch

No really. I lifted a real flaming torch
a grumpy stagehand lit with a giant
lighter as we prepared our entrance.

Shadows flickered against
the scrim before slowly it rose
to reveal Klyttemnestra, wild,

on a stage strewn with crimson
light. I guided her with my
fire. She followed with
her gaze.

Really not all discordant
families murder each other
they divorce. A different
kind of death like I died once

in a court enforced order over
temper. I was carrying a torch
for a heart-throbbing redhead then.

Electra, daughter deranged, undomestic,
and berserk in blood dies: until the family's
final bows. Waiting where I stood
in my odyssey onstage, my eyes were peeled

for the covert red light to cue our exit,
we're done. All the while
Klyttemnestra, Electra, Orestes and Chrysothemis
bow and bow,
audience aflame, stomping, whistling,
rip-roaring real acclaim.

Onomatopoeia of a Sister

Sorella, is the satiny sound Italian siblings say. The word
for sister, *Ah-Choht* in Hebrew sounds stalwart. While
ah-thel-fee binds Greek sisters weaving and swaying an
ancient line dance. The word in French, *sœur,* the sound
that conjures-up a caress and chimes family esprit.

My friend says the English word: sister, *Sisss - t- e r —*
spat between top two teeth, snips and snarls all esses
that hiss with a bite of tee we never get to choose.

In my childhood I dreamt this title was a tender term.
I sobbed for it. Summoning esses of solace, soothing,
sympathy. She would be my darling angel, a booster,
my family. She would come to me anywhere anytime.
I made up her smile and talked to her hour after hour
in solitude when my mother forgot to bear more babies
than me.

Sixteen Turned Backward

esses
arms
to toes I'm a
left
foot song
seeking advice
things
swerve
ask
something
else
a slinky
slide
a sincerely sung
hip
hugging slow
foxtrot
success essing

unexpressed
in spasms
salvos
of silence
stunted
in shimmies
summer
the silly
season
when I ask
see
me
don't see me
so
six
teen

Mark Morris: Paul Hindemith,
Kammermusik No. 3

Pacific Northwest Ballet

That moment even air
        held its breath
                violins loosened bows,

horns shook out slaver,
the undertow of the cellos
umber sound rested vibrations
like ghosts set loose
        the moment suddenly
            the dancers danced
                a cappella.

Had it been a vocal concert
it would have been
        a Gregorian chant
           or a cantor's alleluia
               offering an old ceremony
causing the devout to renew
vows to God.

We made vows to art
it was all about art,
this silence
        and dancers
           moving, weaving
              against the backdrop
of silence, steady,
in the silence

of their own accompaniment.
   and then
although we didn't see,
         the pit musicians lifted
            their work so dominant
               cords shimmered over us
and dancers
     walked into skips
        skipped into runs ran
          into jumps
             and leaping flew

extending arms, legs, toes

catapulting an existence
religiously exaggerated
until we couldn't
        sit,
          couldn't stand
             to sit still.

Acts of Dumb Love Everywhere

Tales of Hoffmann

If they were my arms I would
reach around to engulf
the love-sick troubadour feverishly
kissing not noticing she's

a mechanical doll until her parts
and pieces litter the stage.
Like me do you wish he'd
apprehend, in another act,

the singer he loves
has been forbidden to sing,
and she does sing, for him, and dies
the moment he arrives?

Another act, I'd whirl
limbs wildly waving him off
the finagling Venetian
courtesan stealing

his reflection, laughing
at him oaring on love's green canal.
Like I am are you in love
with Hoffmann's lyrical arias?

Assuming they were my arms I would tender
them around Jacques Offenbach,
as he lay dying three months before
his beloved opera ever opened,

and benevolent muse, will you
extend your arms, wrap me rock me
when I leave the stage?
Hoffman's washed his hands

of love, spends time lifting a pint
telling stories of his life while you
and I, muse, wildly sing his songs with love
until parts and pieces of music litter the stage.

Destiny's Obbligato Perseveres

Oh destiny, your rhythmic formula's airborne,
bearded and undulating above me, the day

the moving van from Minnesota loses its way.
Destiny, thank goodness, you are fated to persevere

under muggy skies. In awe I look up
unaware you signal me in a mysterious

leitmotif as I see —*the mountain's out*.
I walk to Dick's Drive-in

to find a phone to call for the key, my family,
bored, sticky in hot shirts and shorts, wait.

Oh Destiny, you must have been waiting
nearby, savoring the seven years

that passed until we would meet.
That day, airing out the humidity

you probably opened hatches
and attached lifelines sailing

your boat through the Ballard Locks.
Fate and Destiny were destined to be lovers.

So they threw me a curve. The family
moved in then out. Children

followed their passions
their father followed who knows what. Leaving

me with the house key, open doors,
empty rooms and an outcome unknown.

Did you and I brush shoulders
in Belltown's noon crowd? Was I looking

down adding the tip to my tab
when we sat next to each other

on stools at the Pike Place Fish'nChips?
Oh destiny you knew.

Probably after one rainy Sunday
we were destined to pull up side by side

at the Pink Elephant car wash on Denny and 6th.
Unknowing, though fated, do you think

if you'd seen me you'd have walked into
a lamppost or fallen on your face predestined

to step from the curb tripped up —
the way Beethoven's motif in his *Fifth*,

induces a vortex in an obbligato
of Fate? Before Fate became *our tune*

I welcomed you spiraling in awe toward
the dazzle of my irresistible smile.

The Reason We Keep Secrets

The ambrosia beetle makes holes,
chews trees silently. The pinholes

suck in rainwater to configure
layers so no two maples

are alike when sliced a thirtieth
of an inch thick for veneer.

Figured-ash veneer looks like eyes,
measled-walnut, like lips.

Satinwood is smooth like a good talker
inviting fingertip caresses.

Pearwood and wenge are mysterious.
A facade of veneer hides substrate,

top layer of intricate inlay obscures paradox.
No two husbands are alike.

The children ask about their father,
the husband who came before the present

husband, the one whose death
left a coil of personas hidden

under flitches of falsehoods. Layers
deeper than the silence of insomnia nights

below the story never learned.
What can I say? I worry,

chewing over Voltaire's adage,
"The secret of being boring is to tell everything."

Today's husband works wood, veneers his layers
delicately polishing with his hands all he touches.

He sorts and counts to join grains
verbose as fretwork.

You Sing in Your Sleep Too

Study silence and notice:
coloratura swallows, the drone
of the dryer downstairs. In the quiet,

next door someone's hammering, along with
a repeating bleat of a backing truck, the grumble
of a single-engine sea plane. There's the old

refrigerator's quiver. Sometimes
a crow punctuates the lull.
On the back walk in the sunlight I see

sparrows flocked and hold my breath
trying to keep silent, but I exhale.
They hear me, they feel

the sound, a different breath of wind,
for they lift, pivot and disappear.
You tell me you can't stand quiet.

Accompany yourself with radio, TV
and your own voice speaking to no one.
Are you afraid you are alone

without sound? Come.
Come out into the morning sun.
I will sing you birdsongs

whisper their names in your ear
and when you turn
the faint volume of your breath
will brush my lips.

Say I Love You, Don't Say I Love You, He Says I Love You, He Says He Doesn't

Silence is safer.
Not like yesterday when the waterfall of my own
voice unbottled devoured silence by failing to
sit tight till my wishing penny completed its fall,
heads or *tails*. My bellow broke silence lined
with cotton, wool and lace, a silence spacious as time.

We say "He finally broke his silence" as if silence
were an object to be smashed.
Do we ever say he broke his noise?

We expect the company of noise because silence
can have terrible weight.

I waited for the outcome of the sibylline coin.
Shouting "Bite your tongue, balance on
that swell of desire keep silent at the risk of
breaking your heart."

Since yesterday, like forever, I have waited unshushable
washing disquietude away.
Because the coin landed. I bellowed.

So Very Married

We'll be close as pages in a book
My love and I
    —from *Up In Central Park*,
        lyrics by Dorothy Field, 1945

An ordinary Friday when I think I know/
but no.
How would I know how

it feels to be me
if I was / were you? And you?
I encounter you

astonisher / droner.
Would I know, ever,
what moves / arrests you?

Redundant as blinks and clock ticks /
jolting as lightning and alarm clocks.
Your heart / lungs incline.
Supple your spine.

Do I know / ever would I know
what inflames / soothes you?
You bolt from the blue / same again / again.

You know / hot my breath,
I / your skin, by more than
/ imagination,

so would / do I / know how
it feels being you?
Not more / not less real

haphazard / consistent

sameness of sameness
we're a very married

collision of waves
in choppy sea / old
pages snuggled with curled corners

as in / the coat
is wearing me
and soap rejoices in its froth.

His Letters

Well, did you hear how Keats ruminates
on the big picture —all this conjecture
about the *Mansion* and *Doors opening*
as we age, World of misery, Heartbreak, Pain, then

Sense of Beauty overcoming and obliterating it all? He
thinks so loud.
He erupts all over you —but now you're imagining

the mall with its music identical
in the grocery or the dentist. Speakers
ineludable on rafters and walls.
Keats says *Tradesmen . . . say everything*
is worth what it will fetch. Silence. Silence is the pure
       state.

Ask Keats how to put silence into words.
Silence is your whole self
existing in space —and beyond. From my
view the silence of planets ordains their elegance.

Now I'm told that the sound the speed
of light between planets makes
is a roar, careening
like an overwrought gargoyle. Do you wonder
like I do

if Keats is telling us when doors open
the beauty of the *big picture*
is the act of listening?

Four

The Wagner Problem

*All religions must be tolerated. . . for every man
must get to heaven his own way.*
—Frederick the Great

Before Wagner's
Ring Cycle,
before that ritual
ruckus settling on
cerise silk, jewel
of foyer fashion,
before
painting on
a public face,
eyeliner, lipstick,
heels with straps,
I fantasize my defense
to extinguish the family
theological conflagration.

Parking's reserved
and a table
at *le Prelude,*
before a regal ascension
up the lobby's
red-carpet staircase, heart
of audiences' grand entrances.

Before blinking lights,
long lines
at the ladies' loo.
I stash bubbe's
hand-me-down embroidered
hanky in a borrowed
black-beaded opera bag.

Before
toe tromping *excuse-me's*
and *I'm-sorry's*
over laps to seats mid-row,
the sneeze,
the cough,
the program
slipping to the floor.

Dim to dark,
before the conductor,
the applause,
that voodoo unsecured —
Never arrive adorned
in gold as Wagner
levitates above
his unremitting anti-
Semitism
and the Third Reich's embrace,
a cataclysm
that happened
long before
Wagner's *Ring* begins
over aisle E, row T.

Escalating within an immense
naked consciousness
into the axis
of fallible
affairs and glittering
ineptitudes, one by one
I slip away
my jewels of Jewishness
in exchange for the bass-baritone,

Norse god of light,
air and wind. I mute

the offkey cadence
of my flesh
and blood kin
to bare myself
before Wotan's *Valhalla*,
his apogee of looted gold.

We Don't Sing Carols in Our House

Came slowly to me,
how I loved
the songs and worried
not a wit
about the occasion.
I savored
a sleeping baby—
couldn't resist
almost
a baby myself.
Calm, bright, Silent, Night
Misunderstood
manger. Rocking to and fro I
sang and sang
vibrations of melodies
filling me out.
My mind's eye
saw *gifts'* shiny boxes,
really bright *stars*, and
the word swaddle,
even when
I didn't understand
swaddle
I mused
soothing and safe.
Oh Relish the
singing.
Never knew
anything
of the conceit,
of The God.

Above and Below *Tannhäuser's* Proscenium Precipice

> *Tannhäuser dies as pilgrims arrive with news of a miracle: the Pope's staff, which they bear, has burst into bloom.*

While counting my entrance cue perched
far above *Tannhäuser* who thrills in unholy
embraces in *Venusburg* below, I puzzle

over life's seasons and the way
cold temperatures
mean bad news for blossoms.

My life began like an old
coat buttoned tight
over a flowered dress

of soft silk charmeuse.
Now the base of my spine
quivers with Wagner's

lush opening themes.
I'm devoured
by crescendos,

forcing heat
to rise in shock waves
when *Tannhäuser* seeks

absolution in the first act
as he collides bedeviled
by his opposing delights.

From this height I muse on
questions of life's progression.
Some say it's a gene

that senses timing is right
for blossoms to open.
None of us knows for sure

when flowers
will bloom, constrained
by too cool nights,

too little rain or a dearth of lullabies.
Maybe it was my family
trading blows in the first act

of my birth. Or maybe,
just a gene caused
me to silently flunk ABC's

and never master
numbers. It may have been
the slow grind, uphill.

Blossoms,
of late-bloomers' blossoms,
are brilliant.

I'm a *Grace* waiting for a cue,
swirling in gut-feelings of nature
seeded to my old life. Adorned

in diaphanous tulle,
luminescent in the harmony
of a woodwind choir

and the brass offstage
I descend toward *Venusberg's*
orgies, when violins and cellos

catch air
to billow my veils.
Measure by measure I meet

two other *Graces* manifest
as a motif under accent lights
flooding us in beams of spring.

We're Goddesses of charm,
beauty and creativity.
Silent of course, like

any painting.
Our finger-tips touch. We
endure the entire act

balancing a world's fatigue
on the open-petal pattern
of our lifted arms.

There's No Right Way to Do This Wrong

The average kill date
for flowering plants is
November 11th
explains the gardening guru
in the morning news.
He says, pot
them up, cut them back
by half, bring them in
to a bright room.

Yet, I know
all the light
in the universe
won't keep us
from dying.
I can see you bringing
tenders
of hospice
and family
into a room
of vintage green-leaf
wallpaper like mine
after the doctor

comes himself
to that room
to explain
the waning season.
Of course
I will have
mis-heard
the doctor's
forecast, and order
fresh seeds, new
soil.

A Cool Hand Settles the Score

Full heavily of sorrow would I sing.
—Samuel Taylor Coleridge

Watching him score *Dialogues*
of the Carmelites

I compose myself, in French.
My heart's the instrument
Poulanc is fingering.
Note by note an oboe streams
breath on inspiration into
lobes of lung in minor keys.
One dissenting voice,
pulse of Poulanc's orchestra,
its rests and its themes
float like a ribbon
in and out of ears

notwithstanding ahead
a dozen beheadings.

An open warning to Abess *Mother Marie*
step by step,
and sweet *Sister Constance of St. Denis*
whose song petals spring
to *Blanche de la Force's* penultimate
choice to join, red-flagged, up

the plank —
sings, step, sings, step, sings.

Can you think
how it feels
the moment before
in the heart of the composer?
The thump

bifurcating vertebras
and tightly interlaced
muscles once attaching
the plainchanting tongues
Poulanc scores
descending
on a five line stave,
our nuns'

last timbre,
heart felt *Ave*?

Ploys, Plots, Extravaganza, and Then
Boris Godunov

Mute I heft heavy a tricolor banner. Eclipsed
but euphoric surrounded by seismic tones
of basso-profondos, sultry contraltos and cool
currents of the soprano section's lyric. Singers
gooey with makeup widening eyebrows and lips
soar above coronation horns, kettle drums and clappers
on chimes, raise dust onstage where lives don't always end
as we wish. *Boris'* grandeur lives four hours his hot
and cold reign four acts. Woven gold threads of tightly
strung fabrications and onyx eyes of subterfuge glitter
driven by the fanfare,
a history

of tzar-tangled murders and mystics as peasant's grease-
painted wattled skin serve a fresh faced daughter. We
   embrace
the *Simpleton* in his tolling lament wary of *Grigori,*
a conniving *Pretender,* and *Marina* the ambitious
Polish Princess. Tension tightens the audience obscured
below, yearning to shout out: "Beware
unctuous *Prince Shuiski,*" as *Boris* hallucinates the ghost
of the dead *Demitri* in stage air thick with music's prickly
   heat
and goose bump cold.

Grand—
the zenith of opera. When the end comes, I don't
know it's the final finale
hiding my face in the hood of a ratty robe.
My unknowing last shimmering moment on an opera stage.
Time stuck in something about death.

I'll miss Mussorgsky's dissonance I'll miss abandoned
mind-muddled *Boris* as bells: toll rolling toll warning.
Don't take me away don't tear apart viscera of my heart
to cool in time's dissolving minor-scale.
leaving nothing.
Now the curtain drops, silence rises.

Robert Davidson, Trapeze Dancer

You fly and I am you.
Your right hand
locks on your trapeze
mine curls

tight in my pocket.
Like heart beats
from stage right
drums and flutes. You fly
buoyed in blue air
I know how it feels to die.

Stagelight strobes your eyes
flashing cellophane stars
extruding a limb of light
to me. I look out
through your eyes.
Magnetized I am you.

We are a jaguar
swooping. We
levitate silently
from prehistoric tarpits
of ordinary life to dance
a pas-de-deux
and I am you

until you smile
in the bow light
embracing applause.
My hands sting,
widow of feats
of association.

The Chambers in Symphony Hall

The crush in the lobby is alive with life and death
debates: Brahms vs Bruckner, tempo and temper.
Before lights blink you illustrate the essence of life,

gesturing how our heart is connected to the ups
and downs of our diaphragm;
how each breath moves our heart.

This body of work scored
for two keyboards is relentless
with certainty, thrusts rhythm

into the air. My body serves
two masters when the imperious
chords of a sixteenth note

octave surge and oxygen
vital as melody heaves through my
respiratory tract conducting air

filled with grace notes
into my bronchial tree
snagging breath in hidden surfaces

on the little pockets of my lung.
Nowhere in the body
does the outside world

with all its creatures of microscopic
dimension have such easy access
to the sacred interior cavities.

Inhaling the climax of the main theme
the nubile rhythm undulates
my diaphragm, dances my heart

suspended in its pericardial sac. Fine-
tuned, senses stand erect in organic synthesis
as I exhale the entire cosmos of my life.

Super numerary

The best thing about being a Super is that the voice is
banished. Eye on the conductor, alert to the orchestra,
the Super's voiceless character onstage exists in make-
believe. At the climax ovation bravos are received for
the stars' sublime singing continuing to glow even
after stars depart and I emerge from the back corner
and bow. I don't leave. I won't leave. I stay on stage
triumphant subsumed by warm swells of vibration's
molecules still spilling along the opera house walls
bouncing against balconies and chandlers, flying to
the stage from the audience's empty red seats. Echoes
of adulation gush over me after they all retire: stage
manager, conductor, musicians, chorus, principals,
electricians, prop crew, makeup and costumers. After
stagehands sweep-up and stow the full moon in the flys
the lights flick out, door locks click. Celestially lit in
hurdy-gurdy enchantment I grow taller standing, feet
apart, on the proscenium arms raised sky-high seeing
everything. Just me.
Here I stand, still.

Notes

("*Ida LaGray* Explicates How Long Love Can Last
Before It Is Severed")

Opera, *Andrea Chénier*: based on the life and death
of the poet who was guillotined at the end of the
the French Revolution. Composed by Umberto
Giordano. First performed 1896 *Ida LaGray* is a
silent character, considered to have truly existed,
who was released and lived when "*Maddalena
(Chénier's lover) bribes the jailer Schmidt to let her
change places with a condemned noblewoman.*"

national razor a term for Guillotine

(Dear Director, It's *Werther* This Season)

Opera, *Pelléas et Mélisande*: Claude Debussy.
The French libretto adapted from Maurice
Maeterlinck's symbolist play. Opened in Paris
April 30, 1902.

Opera, *Werther*: Jules Massenet. Opened February
16, 1892.

Light-walking. Stand-ins for the singers, during
tech week, are directed place to place on stage
while the director sets the lights.

(The Prop Bag Needed a Body)

Opera, *Rigoletto*: Giuseppe Verdi, Italian liberto by
Francesco maria Piave, based on a play by Victor
Hugo. Opened March 11,1885.

Lily Pons, 1898-1976 French-American popular
coloratura soprano.

chutes: closed area offstage leading into the wings
on either side of the stage.

(Madama Butterfly's Mother)

Opera, *Madama Butterfly*: by Giacomo Puccini,
Italian libretto by Luigi Illica based on a true event
that occurred in Nagasaki in early 1890's. Opened
February 17, 1904.

(Suzanne and I Were Cast)

Opera, *The Daughter of The Regiment*: an opera
comique by Gaetano Donizetti. French libretto, by
Jules-Henri Vernoy de Sant-Georges and Jean-
Francois Bayard. Opened February 11, 1840.

(Lights Out, Curtain Closed, It Begins)

Opera, *Das Rhinegold*: the first and shortest of the
four operas in Richard Wagner's Ring Cycle.

"...leave everything / in the lighted world behind"
quoted from Sue Elliott, Director of Education,
Seattle Opera.

(I Carried a Torch)

Opera, *Electra*: one act opera by Richard
Strauss. German language libretto by Hugo von
Hofmannsthal. Opened in Dresden January 25,
1909.

(The Relatives in My Libretto)

"Swinging On a Star" from movie, *Going My Way*,
Jimmy VanHeusen and Johnny Burke, 1944.

"Hey good lookin" Cole Porter, *Something for the
Boys*, 1943.

"Poor Jud is Dead" and "Many a New Day,"
from *Oklahoma*, Richard Rogers and Oscar
Hammerstein, 1943.

"My Defenses Are Down" from *Annie Get Your Gun*,
Irving Berlin, 1946.

"Mairzy Deoats," Milton Drake, Al Hoffman,
Jerry Livingston 1943.

(Acts of Dumb Love Everywhere)

> Opera: *The Tales of Hoffmann* or *Les Contes
> d'Hoffmann*: composed by Jacques Offenbach. First
> performed in Paris 1851. The acts are sometimes
> done in different order by opera companies.

(So Very Married)

> "Close as Pages in a Book," song from *Up In Central
> Park*, lyrics by Dorothy Fields, music by Sigmund
> Romberg. Opened January 17, 1945.

> "soap rejoices in its froth." from *Soap*, Francis
> Ponge

(Above and Below *Tannhäuser's* Proscenium Precipice)

> Opera, *Tannhäuser*: Richard Wagner. Opened
> Dresden, October 19, 1845

> *"Tannhäuser dies as pilgrims arrive with news of a
> miracle: the Pope's staff, which they bear, has burst into
> bloom"* Edited description of the end of the opera,
> *Tannhäuser*, by John W. Freeman, "Stories of the
> Great Operas" It describes how *Tannhäuser* seeking
> redemption received it, but too late to save his soul.

(A Cool Hand Settles the Score)

> Opera, *Dialogues des Carmélites*: Francis Poulenc.
> Opened Teatro all Scala, Milan, 1957 (in an Italian
> translation). French version opened the same year.
> Based on historical events.

(Super numerary)

Super, from, supernumerary actor. Individuals who are cast to take on a character in non- speaking roles in operas.

About the Author

After her background as a modern dancer, artistic director of a small dance troupe and teacher to adult non dancers for ten years, Carol Levin studied acting at the American Conservatory Theater. Her acting led her to writing and to the Alexander Technique.

Levin's poems have been widely published in journals and anthologies, print and online, in Russia, New Zealand and the US. They have been set to music by singer composer Carol Sams and performed by several chorales. As former Literary Manager for The Art Theater of Puget Sound she collaborated with a Russian theater director from Vladivostok, Leonid Anisimov and his translator, Laura Akhmilovskia in translating and producing Anton Chekhov's four major plays, as well as compiling and translating a dictionary of Stanislavski terms.

Carol Levin's previous poetry collections are, *Stunned By the Velocity, Red Rooms and Others* and *Sea Lions Sing Scat*. She is an Editorial Assistant at the venerable journal, *CrabCreek Review* and she teaches The Breathing Lab/Alexander Technique, in Seattle, Washington.

Afterword

*May this building bring us many cultural advantages and
make it possible for all to gather here to nourish their souls
with the best of music and the wonder of pageantry.*
> —Mayor Bertha K. Landes on the
> dedication of the cornerstone of
> Seattle Center Opera House,
> May 18, 1928.

And indeed the full fruition of Mayor Landes wish came to pass.
> —Carol Levin

CPSIA information can be obtained at www.ICGtesting.com
Printed in the USA
LVOW11s2154040914

402552LV00005B/350/P